For Nick

Like yellow like flying

Jo Peters

All very Best Jo

For Alex and Juliet

© Copyright Jo Peters 2019

Published by Half Moon Books 2019
An imprint of OWF Press Community Interest Company,
Otley Courthouse, Courthouse Street, Otley, West Yorkshire LS21 3AN

www.owfpress.com

All rights reserved. No part of this book may be copied, reproduced, stored in a retrieval system or transmitted, in any form or by any electronic or mechanical means without the prior permission of the copyright owner.

ISBN 978-1-9993036-3-1

Printed and bound by ImprintDigital.com, UK

Acknowledgements

Hurdle-maker won first prize in the *Grey Hen Competition 2017* and is published in *Songs for the Unsung*, ed. Joy Howard (Grey Hen Press, 2017).
Not just words is published in *Hippocrene – Poems of Nature and the Spirit*, ed. Mervyn Linford (Littoral Press, 2017).
Night shift won second prize in *The Red Shed Competition 2015*.
The boy who loved birds was published in *ARTEMISpoetry* (Issue 19, 2017). It also appears in *Hippocrene – Poems of Nature and the Spirit*, ed. Mervyn Linford (Littoral Press, 2017).
Host appears in *The Ver Prize 2018* (Ver Poets, 2018).
Like yellow like flying is published in *Hippocrene – Poems of Nature and the Spirit,* ed. Mervyn Linford (Littoral Press, 2017).
Suffragettes was published in *Pennine Platform* (No. 74, 2013).
Keith Douglas was published in *Acumen* (No.64, 2009).
Appearances won second prize in the McCarthy and Stone *View from a Window* competition 2017.
Goddess was published in *Surprise View – Poems about Otley* (Otley Word Feast Press, 2015). The poem also appears in the poetry play, *Town Below the Steps* by Matthew Hedley Stoppard et al (Half Moon Books, 2017).
Espere Verde was published in *ARTEMISpoetry* (Issue 10, 2013).
Sea song was published in *Running Before the Wind*, ed. Joy Howard (Grey Hen Press, 2013).
my grandmother's house was published in *The Book of Love and Loss*, ed. June Hall and R. V. Bailey (Belgrave Press, 2001).
It's not that I don't believe in ghosts was published in *Orbis* (Orbis 182, 2017).

With thanks to members of Otley Poets and Otley Stanza for their advice and support. Also thanks to the Half Moon Books team and most of all to Jane Kite for her invaluable help and insight when putting this collection together.

Contents

Ferns	1

folk, flocks, and flowers

Hurdle-maker	5
Catherine Wordsworth 1808-1812	6
Not just words	7
We are looking for frogs	8
Night shift	10
The boy who loved birds	11
Bulbs	12
Botany field trip	13
Host	14
Favourites	15
Like yellow, like flying	16
Sweet peas	18
Suffragettes	19
Keith Douglas	20
Appearances	21
more snow later I reckon	22
The Adoration of the Shepherds	23
Bells, parables and psalms	24
Stream	26
pathetic fallacy	27
Goddess	28

Tide be runnin' the great world over

Keeping one's distance	32
Shells, Malaga beach	33

Espere verde	34
Malaga voices	35
Sea song	36
Seascape with figures	37
Things past	39
Found and lost	40
Tipping point	41

trying to unweave unwind unravel

Saturdays	47
Sonnets from a foreign country	49
1. A strange man	49
2. Exclusion	50
3. First garden	51
4. Likes and dislikes	52
5. Lessons	53
6. Because it's Christmas	54
my grandmother's house	55
Bequest	56
Latin at the Marist Convent	57
on the lolly assembly line	59
In bed with Shakespeare	61
Reading Macbeth at night	62
Stepfather	63
The rest is silence	64
Perfection	65
Time	66
Father	68
It's not that I don't believe in ghosts	69

Ferns

I see maidenhair spleenwort's neat scrawl
on the wall, trace the new curves
of polypody's foot-fingers till I come back
to the beginning, while buckler fern unfurls,
spreads its elegant airy shuttlecock.
Soft shield fern stalks, furry with rust,
are now topped by spirals showing the green, just.
Hart's tongue unrolls its shining narrow scrolls,
and all the wood becomes a world of whorls,
curls, coils of miniature cellos.

folk, flocks, and flowers

Gerard Manley Hopkins

'folk, flocks and flowers' is from Gerard Manley Hopkins' poem:
'Duns Scotus's Oxford'

Hurdle-maker

I take the cart to the heath
for hazel boughs,
then to the river,
cut willow withies.
My errands of mercy.

I lay my hazels, man length,
weave withies, bind tight.
My works of mercy.

They must be strong,
my hurdles,
my cradles of mercy.

I called our daughter Mercy.
Born a few summers past,
not like me,
she's a one for talk.
Sets herself down in the yard
to watch my merciful work.
Leaves off trailing fingers
in shavings,
points at hurdles
stacked by the wall,
demands: *What for?*
She'll not understand
my woven work of mercy
for the soon to be dead.
God help me –
To take sick people to the monks
is what I said.

Hurdle: A frame or sledge on which traitors used to be drawn through the streets to execution

Catherine Wordsworth 1808–1812

You creep into my study while I work,
and play contentedly beside the hearth.
Today you croon a blithe and wordless song
to your best stones, intent as you place them
here and there upon the patterned rug.

In this house so full of talk, your words
are few though you will soon be four.
Your shiny coinage: smiles, mischief, mirth,
and beguilements particularly yours,
so all who come are charmed and seek you first.

Like starlings in a tree the children chatter,
and run ahead outdoors while you soon tire.
Your mother holds the babe so I lift you
shoulder high when we walk to the lake,
your hair so fine it tickles my cheek.

But now you sense my eyes on you and laugh,
pretend to hide behind my chair, peep out.
I've had sufficient versing for this morning.
Come, take my hand, my little Chinese maiden,
we'll go and find Aunt Dorothy in the garden.

It is now believed that Catherine, the Wordsworths' fourth child, had Down's Syndrome which was not identified as a medical condition until 1866. So the Wordsworths and their friends simply saw Catherine as a delightful and somewhat unusual child

Not just words
Written on reading that many words referring to the
natural world have been removed from the latest edition
of the Oxford Junior Dictionary

Was there a committee in charge of de-naturing,
of displacing, disconnecting, unseasoning?
Whichever sharp-suited young employee of OUP,
deputed to de-clutter, de-flower from A to E,
scythed a swathe of bluebells and buttercups,
sprayed all the dandelions and cowslips.
Was it you who deleted adder and acorn,
who cancelled conker (conker!) cygnet and catkin?

Say acorn, you have the curve of a light brown nut,
miniature egg, snug in rough-to-touch cup,
a pixie pipe. You have shades of Autumn woods
where jays squawk and squirrels hide winter food.
You have ancient oaks, seasoned beams for a house,
a solid family table, pannage, the Mary Rose.

We are looking for frogs

is written in a five-year-old hand
above a drawing turned up in an old folder.
Felt-penned in blue we stand on our stick legs,
labelled in orange: Juliet Dad Alex Mum.
Not at our feet – we don't have them –
but at the bottom of the page
swarm a host of tiny frogs.
They too are penned in orange
but I love the brio
of their sketchy depiction. Eyes
of course, on heads, bodies and some legs.
They seem to move.

A misty memory rises of a wood after rain,
perhaps in Scotland. Hundreds of minute frogs
had chosen this damp day to abandon a watery lifestyle
and we saw them scramble and stumble on new legs
in the strange elements of land and air,
surprising themselves
with the occasional leap.

We are static in the picture
but enlivened by very smiley mouths,
Dad's only a little less so.
What could she know?
Our snowman arms project at right angles
from our triangular bodies. Probably by accident
Dad and Mum are nearly holding
alien four-fingered hands.

One unremembered long caravan summer evening
she had taken such care to differentiate us,
our hair particularly. Mum and Juliet
have straight lines, Alex's curls a joined e pattern
around his head.
But Dad is a triumph of portraiture.
She has caught the bushy compensatory tufts
over his ears, the bald central area represented
by four blue hairs.

She preserved the day as a photo never could;
our frail symmetrical family together
with a lot of small frogs in a wood.

Night shift
after Seamus Heaney

Had I not been so tired I'd have missed you,
but I went to bed early in the June dusk
when you were just setting about your business.

A bird with a face gliding low over meadow grasses;
a white shadow, quartering the field, listening.
From my window I felt the spell of your industry.

You came and you went so unexpectedly,
now black against a fading sky, wings
stark triangles, something small in your talons.

The boy who loved birds
i.m. Harold Fox 1945–2007

My brother died in a dismal rented flat.
Last summer in the city's stuffy heat
his heart broke and he died there quite alone,
but for a barn owl and the starkest porn.
He'd disappeared, thought to be moving house,
his precious things in store, just that glass case
to keep the past with him. That eager boy,
obsessed with birds, had seen one summer day
the half-crown owl among the bric-a-brac,
bought it, opposed by all, a good day's work.

The phone that rang and rang – 'He's moving house'
we said with truth, and now I say, 'Oh please
can birds, not angels swoop his new abode?'
That kind and funny man, he can't be dead.
What use his wit, his learning, wasted on
winged po-faced angels with no use for wine.
He loved danger, would risk the wild and rough
to bring our mother eggs, braved dizzy cliffs
despite the sharp-beaked gulls, sea far below.
Her death made him more fragile than we knew.

In an old-fashioned bird book we once read:
'Swifts scream exultantly', and commented
on anthropomorphism and new research.
In headlong flight swifts scream to keep in touch,
it seems. Our radar failed; he won't return.
The swifts, they'll soon race overhead again;
their switchback glory ride, their blue-black gleam,
their arrogance and mystery, scream his name.
I dread their cries. They'll tell of death, alone,
a week dead with his owl and that shrill phone.

Bulbs

Under the papery skin
they are hard to my fingers.
They fizz with sap, are
sharpening the swords of spring,
brewing pale petals.

I put them in the cold hole,
in the territory
of the blunt sliding worm,
slow trawl of roots.

Rain will seep down –
lick these small brown bombs
that tick in silence
till they are detonated
by the sun's sputtering fuse.

I tread down the earth;
I am burying death.

Botany field trip

How can anything so lovely
possibly be called bogbean?

The flowers thrust from the dark tarn
that sends back their purity in ripples.
Frilly as expensive underwear,
each a snowflake
hybridised with a Christmas star,
buds held up above the flowers
tinged with the dark pink of nipples.

Floundering inelegantly in water,
we try to persuade them to yield
something of their mystery,
their evanescence,
to cameras and magnifiers,
trudge back, avoid with blunt boots
an arrogance of orchids,
an innocence of bird's eye primroses,
a heartache of butterwort.

We sit, sated with difference,
eat sandwiches in the sun.
Someone idly knocks a pebble
against a stone.
Splitting, it reveals a fossil club moss
hidden for three hundred million years.
The magnifiers come out again.

Host

An army is stranded under trees,
bugles echo over water,
pennants flutter in the soft wind.

A pale glory of angels descends,
flickers among mossy rocks,
salutes the sunshine with trumpets.

Yellow flowers open wide the door,
bow welcome to Spring,
sprightly, lightly, she flounces in.

Brother and sister walk by the lake
through wind and sun;
later, Dorothy writes her journal.

Favourites
for Helen

I've just seen the first flower you won't see.
They bob up year on year round your birthday.
They grant permission to believe in spring
despite the snow, prove days are lengthening.

In gardens you particularly disliked yellow,
anyway preferred wildflowers, but would allow
these to be among your favourites. I forgot
you'd given me some of your aconite roots.

They ambushed me today with their pink stalks
hooping through the dead leaves like thin necks.
And when I see them raise their heads to show
diminutive green ruffs circling the yellow

I'll say – enough, enough – stop right there, spring –
how will I bear bugle, wood sage, ragged robin?

Like yellow, like flying

My brother Frank when he was four or five
        thought creatures could be divided
into animals, birds and owls. The insects
        and the fish were obviously not of interest.

Classifying, ordering, he had in common
        with the monks who listed God's Creation,
patiently illumined its dignity and beauty,
        in the Twelfth Century Aberdeen Bestiary.

They didn't rate insects either as the bees
        were in with the Birds (and the phoenix),
ants were in with the Small Animals
        (which included the weasels and moles).

We've lost the dragons and the basilisks
        (they were in with the Reptiles and Snakes),
and no other insects were pictured, or listed;
        they have made up a lot of ground since.

Four million species of beetles, unaware
        they are in a Kingdom, a Class and an Order,
and, each dignified with two Latin names,
        scurry on in their mysterious ways.

Dandelions echo the sun's glory in May;
        we have given them a place in the Daisy family,
and their species name *Taraxacum officinale*,
        tags not intrinsic, like yellow, like flying.

It was sad when the pea family became
> *Leguminosae*, such a heavy vegetable name.
Though no longer *Papilionacae*, the butterflies
> on the gorse are just as gold, as bright.

We throw nets over wildness, randomness,
> until all are pinned in line, for the convenience
of *Homo Sapiens*, no longer in praise of God.
> Frank had problems with the hedgehogs.

Sweet peas

My grandmother lived to be very old,
and after she died I always saw her,
small and wispy, sitting in a fug
of fire and smoky joss sticks burnt to mask
the smell of urine. One day, on display,
a crinkled tin-foiled cube of oasis,
and in the gritty foam she'd stuck stiff heads
of daffodils which stared this way and that.
Quavery, enjoying our bright praise,
I made it at the day centre, she said.

There she sat in this undusted, dim
corner of memory, until the year
I coaxed sweet peas from their gun-pellet seeds,
came home to find the sunny garden's air
held tendrils of a light forgotten scent
that held me, pulled me back across the years.
We both ran past our tall grandmother,
my brother first, into the flower tent,
breasting the crowds, the hot and heavy smell
of canvas, crushed grass and a million flowers.

We saw a trestle table with a sign:
'Six Sweet Peas in a Vase', over a flock
of pastel butterflies that, poised for flight,
all angled to admire pale reflections,
sunned themselves in their own scent. But our
eyes gobbled up a red, gold-lettered card.
You've won, Granny, you've won first prize, we yelled.
She shushed us, told us not to make a fuss.
Our eyebrows, at each other, over grins,
said people get a bit odd when they're old.

Suffragettes

In June my sweet peas climb over an arch,
join hands for easy summer to dance through.
Green slender tendril fingers cling and clutch,
flowers undo ruffled petals, soft scent blows.
Demure Edwardian women lightly stroll
with billowing white skirts; pink sashes
tie wide-brimmed hats, while lilac parasols
tilt to preserve pallor, conceal passion.

November frosts flowers, shrivels brown winged leaves,
I struggle to untie tough wiry stalks,
prise tendrils from supports. Hammering hooves
bear down. Pink rubber feed tubes choke.
A late flower lies trampled in the mud;
I collect hard seeds from papery pods.

Keith Douglas
Written on seeing his 'Self-portrait in a steel shaving mirror, England 1944'

You stare at me through unused years
from your self-portrait drawn in war,
look older than your twenty-four,
honed by desert winds and stars.

Light glinted on your mirror's steel,
you saw yourself a handsome chap
with jaunty 'tache and army cap,
only the eyes unnerve, appal.

You gaze at me born 'forty four,
the year that you were killed in France,
reproaching me for each missed chance,
why did I even waste an hour?

You knew you hadn't time to dive,
with bursting lungs and limbs of lead,
and wrench away from their cold bed
the ribbed grey shells with crinkled wave,

to prise apart each tight-clasped shell,
hurl to the sea each fruitless cup,
till soft flesh yields its treasure up
to fingertip, hard-lustred pearl.

Light pencil strokes halted awhile
slow march of wartime's wasted days,
you looked at death with knowing gaze,
your brightness blunted by dull steel.

Appearances
after Louis MacNeice

From an upstairs room it looks as though
a snowdome's been upturned before my eyes.
Beyond a field of yellowing winter grass,
behind a scrawled hedge and three leafless trees
inked on the brown and distant wooded hill,
my gaze is caught and held. I'm mesmerised.
Everything is changing all the time
as I watch the hundreds of white shapes
fall and rise the far side of the trees.

Sun strikes white, a flashing blizzard swirls,
then as they flicker down and disappear
I know that they are gulls; my view alters.
Nothing stays. The trees lose all their starkness.
There's more than trees between snowbirds and me.

more snow later I reckon

hands in armpits   tom hollers   come by nell come by
above snow-swept fell   iced wind drifts   new star
shifts   high steer-by light   nimble sheep trit-trot
nimbus fleece star-bright   the collie stares intent
slinks low   shuffles flock downhill   off the fell

ewes hide lamb-swell in straggled wool   snatch hay
in barn's lee   tonight no swaledales die snow-swaddled

stamping stomping   hill farmers gaze at white dazzle
down-dale   new star   new stare   stony stair
steep stumble towards inn's warmth   lantern light

The Adoration of the Shepherds
After the painting by Caravaggio

A girl woke from exhausted sleep to hear
the voices, questing, breathless, rough with awe,
remembered jolting journey, strangers, fear.
She looked at him asleep upon the straw,
remembered as a distant dream the kind
innkeeper's wife, the pain, how the red hands
had washed her baby, showed her how to wind
white linen round him in tight swathing bands.

They said, 'The angel told us of a child.'
So glad that these plain men could say such things,
as she lifted her baby the girl smiled,
'I saw one too.' Terror of shining wings
was stilled. But in the dark she feared this boy
would bring her more than common pain and joy.

Bells, parables and psalms

It's the sound we hear first, echoing across the steep-sided valley
in these Spanish mountains, as though glockenspiels were tapped randomly,

then we make out small shapes running and leaping on the rocky slopes,
dots stream over barren yellowed ground in time with tumbling notes.

Later that day we meet a shepherd and his flock on our narrow path,
goats silky-smooth, sheep closely fleeced, the colours of rocks and earth.

We stand to one side as they jostle by, plain, blotched and mottled,
young ones bleating, panicky, scrambling after mothers, the air clotted

with their smell, the jongling of their bells, as between the trees they snatch
at tufts of yellowed grass, small new leaves, all nibbling nothing much.

How nimble and skinny these nomadic beasts, how foreign they are,
the multicoloured sheep wilder-looking, skittish, not as sheepish as ours,

floppy-eared goats, horned like devils, with a wilful glint in
their yellow eyes.
Their rebellious demeanour the reason, I suppose, that when
Jesus described

God separating the flock, he chose to send the goats to perish
in Hell
while the obedient sheep, as their reward, trotted off to life
eternal.

Bells fade, the rough-haired shepherd leads his motley flock to
better grazing;
our shepherds drive their sheep, but he inhabits an apt image
of a saviour.

I don't suppose this shepherd would leave all these to find a
single lost one
but he just might. We hear bells later competing with traffic in
the small town,

and look across the road, see him washing down the day's dust
outside the bar,
his flock foraging near the river, the quiet waters by,
nondescript dog on guard.

Stream

When we arrived at Monk's House it was the wrong day
so we did not see your study, your roses, your grave.
In the heat how a thrush shouted with abandon, how politely
a notice rejected us, as we looked at each other as if to say:
What now?
Here words streamed from your pen. Here after all you were happy:
I don't think two people could have been happier than we have been.
Here the voices you had dreaded returned to terrify you:
I can't fight any longer. Here in the threatening wartime spring
German bombers thundered from the sea and over the rounded downs
with the little churches in the hollows. Here dolour, desolation, despair
bowed your head, weighed you down, heavy as stones.

I'm glad we came the wrong day, Virginia. In your house,
surrounded by your particular possessions, how could we not
have imagined you as you put on your coat, your hat, took up your cane,
set out over familiar fields to the river?
You left your hat and your cane on the bank like stories.

pathetic fallacy

on my birthday
I walked alone in the Washburn valley
but the chiff-chaff
practised his hesitant two-finger scale
for me
a few frail windflowers in the wood
blew for me
the curlew in swooping flight
called called called for me
on the wall
bright moss softened the stones for me
celandines shone
their child-painted suns in the hedge
for me
at the edge of the puddles
birds had printed arrows for me
pointing to the narrow stone bridge
that stretched lightly over the stream for me
and a sprightly wren
twirled his staccato rattle
for me
and then dry sticks of last summer's umbels
exploded
starry fireworks for me
all for me

Goddess

Driving, I caught a glimpse
of Botticelli's Venus
wearing blue jeans,
walking over Otley bridge
where the swift Wharfe
had swirled her ashore.

She knows the mill girl
who dawdles by the forge
as the muscled smith
leans his back against
a massive flank to tip
up the feathered fetlock.

She smiles at the lad
herding his flustered sheep
across the bridge,
who will take his thirst
to the barmaid at the Black Bull
when the selling is done.

She sees the nursemaid
in Tittybottle Park turn,
push her charge up the hill
to New Hall where
the gardener's boy once
threw her a rose.

The goddess steps
aside as the young folk,
now uniformed, homework
downloaded, throng up
to Prince Henry's School where
the desire lines of courtship abide.

The invisible wind strews no roses,
but it whips her hair,
her glorious corn-coloured hair
that lifts, streams away
from the perfection
of her oval tilted face.

Tide be runnin' the great world over
Charlotte Mew

From 'Sea Love' by Charlotte Mew

Keeping one's distance

The woman next to him
in the plane is reading 'Offshore'
by Penelope Fitzgerald.
He knew it existed in the penumbra
between truth and lies, like poems.
Like this one. Where they touch
disconcerts, chafes.

They begin the descent.
As they plunge, juddering,
he sees, from this god-like vantage,
a small red fishing boat
peacefully trailing its white wake
towards the slow abrasions
of the beach.

Shells, Malaga beach

Why do I have to collect
these wave-worn pieces
of clams, cockles, scallops?
No one here gives them a glance
as someone or something
has already eaten their owners.

Because the patterns
engage my eye amid
this sandy randomness.

Cockles are ridged
like the weathered tiles
that slope on the city roofs;
gingery permanent waves
have been endlessly turned
by innumerable impermanent waves
on the way to being sand.

Triangles of scallop shell,
ridges widely fanned,
are fins for an orange fish.

Half a white shell curves, a plume
unfurling, the wing of the angel
Gabriel whose swish
surprised Mary in a sunlit room.

Espere verde
Malaga musings in green biro

Have the fluorescent green parakeets always been here?
Have they flown over the sea from Africa?
Is it their livid vivid wings or their jungle calls
that make the palm trees by the beach so exotic?

Will I find again the shop with the green skirt?
Will I navigate by church towers, plazas and bars
through the crammed streets? One so narrow yesterday
I touched houses on both sides, hands on the rough walls.

Anything else green here? Not much. But the blue between
orange roof tiles and the warmth of the sun entice me
to forget green fields. The dark pines as we climbed
to the Moorish castle will do very well for now.

At the road crossing on the way to the harbour
I am instructed in lights to 'ESPERE VERDE.'
I suppose hoping and waiting have much in common.
Yes – I can wait for rain and green.

Malaga voices

The city shouts harsh greetings,
explodes firecrackers and fiestas,
laughs and sings into the warm night.
The city buzzes insistently with Vespas;
impatient horns toss up blasts of sound.
The city counts its time in bells
and the clangs pull in the faithful.

The sea whispers just the same story,
breathing in ... out, as it does at home.
The sea's crisp wavelets shift stones,
sand, shells; smooth, wash and shine.
The sea's breath smooths my edges too
as it sighs back, then teases my feet
again with an inrush of transient foam.

Sea song

I take off my watch,
see last summer's sunshine
printed on my arm.
I am still the small girl
in a trance, trailing a net
along the plashy sea line,
as a fossil shell is imprinted on rock.
I croon tunelessly,
firm ribbed sand on my soles.

Now everything shifts like the sea,
that may dandle me,
toss me treasure or wrack,
will overwhelm me.
The dead like seabirds throng round me.

Seascape with figures

The sky held the same colours as the sea,
and floated huge billows of sandy clouds
with rounded underbellies of slate blue,
flocking out to sea, each smaller still,
the colours deepening, both blue and gold,
till cut off by the sea's hard line of light.

The lovers on the shore watched as the light
danced with the dark out on the troubled sea.
Blue deepened to indigo, and swathes of gold
reflected colours, broke the shapes of clouds.
Nearer the beach, because the wind was still,
wavelets stretched out their circles, sand on blue.

She stared at him, her eyes more grey than blue,
which said they should part now, before the light
returned again to darkness, while they still
remembered love relentless as the sea,
before the indigo storm-threatening clouds
blotted forever those bright lanes of gold.

Still silent they walked on, the gold
and grey of pebbles slipped and grated, blue
and beige, as rounded as the tumbled clouds,
shaped like the ripples where the restless light
flickered on the surface of the sea,
but hard beneath their feet as they stood still.

He looked at her and thought that they might still
hold on to love, for the bright shine of gold
is dulled by use, but worth the same. This sea
and sky that now hold their soft beige and blue
will change as day draws in its rays of light;
tomorrow we'll still gaze at sea and clouds.

She thought they were as different as clouds
and sea. This sky, floating its clouds, is still,
unlike the restless water, and so light,
so airy, and so separate. The gold
and shiny pebbles by the stroking blue
are each unique, repulsing alien sea.

The clouds, which were the sea, which will be clouds,
glowed, as the sea's blue shuffled pebbles still,
altered and smoothed, let gold reflect wet light.

Things past

It doesn't take much; just
a few days in the south west,
where the hills are the right height,
their fields the right shape,
their earth the right colour, the air softer,
where slant light on water
still makes and unmakes the clouds.

Just to see that faded photo, four of us
in a boat, Swallows and Amazons,
my sister in plaits, my brothers, lanky,
dangling feet in creek water lukewarm
and silky with mud.

Just the eldest and youngest left now;
empty bookends.

Found and lost

I kept company with my mother today
as I walked the coast path to Meadfoot,
where she used to stay as a girl.
Seabirds throng, calling like children.
Her girl-ghost scrambles the rockpools,
her shrimp bucket slops seawater.
Plaits sticky, bedraggled from swimming,
her feet gritty in sandshoes, she climbs
the endless steps to Aunt Tina's.

There was a man at the seafront cafe,
in Torquay for his mother's funeral,
filling the awkward hours. He sighed,
She was ninety, but it's hard to lose her.
Later you'll find her again, I said.

Tipping point

Once the moment when a listing ship
could not right itself, tipped,
sank, spewing screams and life rafts.

Then in 1959 in the New York Times
'tipping point' became metaphor
for the moment whites
began to leave
like rats, neighbourhoods
where black people had moved in.

Now scientists seek the tipping points
which will propel the earth
into danger, spiralling climate change.
No life rafts.

Always the worst thing about tipping points
is you cannot tip them back,
and one causes another
and another,
like dominoes. Drought, flooding,
uninhabitable lands,
mass migration.

Later or sooner
the tipping point when more people act on this
than don't
will be too late.

Now certainly not a metaphor,
the weight of that small child
lifted into an overfull boat
will be the tipping point
when they meet
the open sea.

Guardian headline after IPPC report on global warming on October 9th 2018
'Tipping points could exacerbate climate crisis, scientists fear'

trying to unweave unwind unravel

T. S. Eliot

From 'The Dry Salvages', *Four Quartets*, T.S. Eliot

Saturdays

Alone in his sanctum
he savours the quiet afternoon.
Carefully, he attaches goods wagons,
winds the engine almost tight,
watches. It whirrs on course along
the rails, safely round the curves,
under the bridge.

How long the wait had been
before the sound
of that slammed door.

He reconstructs the track;
creates sidings.
Now to decide on coaches
for a passenger train,
choose an engine, set it in motion.

Remembers a brown packet,
unwraps it, reads instructions.
Have I time to make the signal box?
Puts aside the transfers,
sets to work.
Almost assembled, checks his watch.
How fast the hours have run;
time to lock up, go down.

Soon they all return.
No one calls a greeting
but from his study he hears
clattering plates, children squabbling.

He considers coming out, asking:
How was Grandma?
Have you been good? Did you walk
as far as the wood?

What can they be doing?
How loud four children are.

They shout, laugh, hammer open
hazel nuts on the stone scullery floor.

Sonnets from a foreign country

1. A strange man

Enter a boy of three, a girl of four
to see a stranger in the big armchair.
Grandma brought a tea tray then went out.
Their mum, as she talked, seemed different.
They sat at her feet, cautious and wary,
edged closer, touched outstretched corduroy,
then began to climb, felt hairy tweed,
prickly moustache and shiny head. 'He's bald,'
the girl whispered and they both giggled.
'Stop that, get down, behave,' their mother said.
'Don't worry, I don't mind at all,' he smiled.

They married. He seemed to grow cold,
a distant adult that they almost feared,
and never thought to touch, call Dad.

2. Exclusion

A girl, a boy, in a basement kitchen,
shook their cornflakes in a bowl,
feeling grown-up, no one watching,
a different house, sense of exile.
Their mother came down with a treat,
crispy buttered crusts of toast,
from the sunny window seat
that she shared with their new guest.
She'd said to call him Uncle Charlie.
They knew he'd come to live with them,
and knew the crusts a sort of bargain.
They crunched gladly, said 'thanks Mum',
ate crumby bits of happiness
that fell from some strange paradise.

3. First garden

He dug for us four small patches of earth
that sloped to the overgrown raspberry canes,
and small beds by the wall. Between, a path.
The younger two dug holes and looked for stones,
but Harold and I raced down the hill to Woolies.
Stacked seed packets rattled with promises;
buy me, buy me smiled the faces of pansies.
Such tiny seeds, we thought they could be lost,
so we planted them in the small beds by the wall,
excitement signalled by our packet flags.

That evening as we all sat round the table,
he said to Mum: 'Why did the children dig
in my spare earth bed? Oh well, too late now.'
Anticipation died down, lost its glow.

4. Likes and dislikes

I knew my mother had a quiet dislike
of those two cats my stepfather had brought
to their marriage. I loved to see them stalk
the garden softly; I liked them a lot.

Another girl and then another boy.
The six of us moved into a tall house
where the long garden's lawn had grown hay-high,
and waspy apples rotted in the grass.

From the dark hall a metal gong called all
of us to silent meals. I watched him eat
green beans, take the seeds, red-grey and small,
from each green case, and eat them last, apart.
I never dreamt of asking why. Just knew
it maddened me then and it still could now.

5. Lessons

In that wild garden where four children played,
the youngest boy climbed up an apple tree,
got stuck, panicked, and clung on afraid.
Their mum was out, the boy began to cry.
'He'll fall!' The eldest knew to call upon
the one who'd help. He saw his son in tears:
'If he got up he can get down again.'
He turned abruptly and went back indoors.

This man picked the apples every year,
took a wicker basket, placed them gently,
laid them in boxes with pedantic care,
dark-dimpled, plumped with juice and summer-scented,
some glowed with greenness, some were flecked with red.
'You must make sure they never touch,' he said.

6. Because it's Christmas

Fragrance of fir, crackle, hiss in the hearth,
Father in the big armchair feeds the fire.
Soft dip, ripple, shadows from the candles
as Grandma fusses, clamps holders on the tree.
The mother gives out crackers to four children,
who, without thought, point them at someone.
Sharp snaps, the smell of small explosions,
laughter, screams, scrambles for mottoes, prizes.

The eldest girl becomes still, gathers herself
for the hardest moment of the year,
and no one but herself makes her do this.
She knows she must cross the miles of the room
towards the man sitting in the big armchair;
she holds her cracker out to him and smiles.

my grandmother's house

today I butter a slice of toast
push my knife in
right through the hard crust
bring it out clean then
dip it into marmalade
and I'm eight again
in a sunny room where breakfast's set
I'm watching her knife do just that
basking in not being one of four
somehow knowing she was my treat
as I was hers

I smell the lemon verbena's warm scent
see faded watercolours
of Egypt Greece sense the hint
of foreignness adventure
taste an exotic treat
long spaghetti with grated cheese
feel our complicity
in the grown-up thrill of being up late
slapping cards down for Racing Demon
a safe rivalry salted by
the knowledge she too wanted to win

oh – and her hair was waist length
wound in a soft coil deftly pinned
the same colour as mine
greying black
what unconsidered thing that I do now
will one day bring me back?

Bequest

The dream slithers away like a grey cat
slipping behind curtains, just the feel of it
left, comforting, familiar. It is evening time;
we four sit round the old electric clothes drier,
and our mother is reading to us. Just the homely
smell of drying lingers, with the sense of the slow
unravelling of a tale, the need to find out, know
what happened on Kirrin Island, to Robinson Crusoe.

Later, searching for a book, among well-worn spines,
the shadow of the dream returns, faded, undefined,
and I think of the miles of shelves, the multitudes
of characters, imaginary and historied, from Bede
to Waugh, in the houses far apart, of the four
who had listened then, rapt, lost in the old stories.

Latin at the Marist Convent

I met Latin in my teens,
and, in a confusion of change, it was a solace;
logical, neat, its reliability reassuring
when my body seemed suddenly out of my control.
It was also clean-sheet new
in the crumpled tedium of school,
so new we needed another language to master it.
Nouns we'd met but they now had cases,
and we learnt to decline them:
nominative, vocative, accusative,
genitive, dative, ablative.

So *'puer'* (boy) could be declined
without confusion or fear of offence.
The case ending told you everything
you needed to know, whether he belonged to someone,
was the subject of the sentence and called the tune,
or if he was the object (of the girl's affections),
so whatever order the words were in
all relationships were transparent.

The newness was like being in love,
total unfamiliarity, but as if I'd always known it;
new but also incredibly ancient,
and, even more romantically, dead.
No one would use Latin to reproach me,
nor would boys call out in Latin across the street,
'Not tonight, Josephine.'
No one would ever propose in Latin again,
or sing to a child, or tell a story.

Imagine Grace and me paired in class
with a copy of Vergil waiting our turn
to construe the tale of the wooden horse of Troy,
as we let our eyes run ahead and come to the bit
where young boys come running out of the city
to deck the horse with garlands,
and, so painfully adolescent were we,
that we were both possessed by uncontrollable giggles
when we saw the word *'pueri'*,
(boy, nominative case, plural).

on the lolly assembly line

a radio played
heartbeat
why do you miss when
my baby kisses me?
as she diligently filled the lolly moulds
from her jug of sweet liquid

she loved that holiday job
each metal box of lollies
that gradually solidified
as they slowly sailed
through a trough of icy brine
brought her nearer
to the portable record player
she dreamed of taking
to outdoor parties on long summer nights

she steered a full batch
to her school friend Kay
who added stick masts as they froze
then gently pushed them
to the end of the trough
where old hand Dot
cased each icy cylinder
in a paper sheath
shuffled them into boxes
for the clunk of the ice-breathing freezers

'just off to the lav for a fag' said Dot
a lolly log jam
it's my favourite milky ones

'chuck us one Kay'
she peeled it
spun careless on her stool
sucked blissfully
daydreaming of kisses

from nowhere came her boss
white-coated Mr John
(no slacking no eating the product)
she stared at him aghast
imagined humiliating reprimand
the sack
but he looked at her and laughed
turned and went without a word

she bought her record player
treasured it
took it everywhere
but when the batteries ran low
Buddy Holly's love for Peggy Sue
slurred
became slower and slower

In bed with Shakespeare

One night
when scrolling for pop on my wireless
through static and foreign voices,
a BBC accent announced
readings of Shakespeare's sonnets.

I lay in thrall
to wild enchantment of words,
to dangerous grown-up secrets.
A beautiful youth ardently loved,
exhilarating frisson,
in the whispering fifties
when gay was queer.
Dark desire for a woman,
lust's aftermath,
betrayal in a cruel love triangle.

Each week I stole upstairs for these,
my dizzying fix
of obsessive passion,
agony of absence, jealousy,
jagged tear of heartbreak, all raw
and real as any adolescent brooding.

As I lay in the dark with Shakespeare,
I wanted to tell him,
that his love had outlasted centuries
and kings and towers,
for it still burned,
flickering over the ether
straight into my untried heart.

Reading Macbeth at night

Open the book. An owl's cry quivers the woods
as innocent talons prepare to shed blood.
In the house two children sleep upstairs.
The wind rises in the trees; they roar
at the broken roundel of the moon
cracked by swirling branches wildly blown
over that face, the mouth agape with woe.

Pages release their spells of long ago
that creep around the nerves, whisper or shout.
Wholesome daytime's sucked away, seeps out.
Conjured up, invited, evil advances
with quiet steps, offering easy violence.
It is unstoppable and without end.
Look! A gift – 'the handle towards my hand'.

Stepfather

We are close now.
We use brushes for the eye sockets, search
for a kind glance, blow
the soil from his mouth
to get a good word from that gape.

He's in those plots he once dug for us
at the end of our garden.
Pansies flutter again
in purple and yellow velvet.

Without flesh we find him homely
and his bones aren't cold to the touch.
We unroll the pouch for our smallest tools –
reveal that complexity of hands
not for holding.

With our small triangular trowels,
we scrape soil with delicate strokes.
We remove the distance
till we have
the length, the measure of him.

The rest is silence

My world has cracked and all I feel is dread.
I can't catch my thoughts, they fly away
and all I hear is noise inside my head

where once clear reason reigned. I studied, read,
and loved to flash and thrust ideas, today
my world has cracked and all I feel is dread

because the father that I held so dear is dead.
This comes to everyone, but not this way,
and all I hear is noise inside in my head

confusing me, my quick feet turned to lead.
Where once I'd run to act, I weigh and weigh.
My world has cracked and all I feel is dread

to see my mother take that man to bed,
all giggles, whispers. Look – her hair is grey!
And all I hear is noise inside my head

that shouts: 'No woman's true.' I looked to wed
a sweet girl once, that's swirled in disarray,
my world has cracked, and all I feel is dread,
and all I hear is noise inside my head.

Perfection

Furniture piled on furniture, papers, food, trash.
She, the rebel, who'd claimed to be misunderstood,
yet treasured our family's past in this hopeless hoard;
she, whose life had begun to swirl out of her control,
shored herself up, to make the unbearable bearable.

But I was not ready for the melons carefully placed,
crowding every already crammed and cluttered surface.
Yellow and green, they bobbed on the kitchen sill,
some lopsided and collapsed, punctured mini beach balls.
Some mouldered on the table, black-spored, oozing, squat.
They filled the house with a sweet jungle stench of rot.
On our paired, stacked family chairs on upside down nests
of hessian, there now reposed three black circles of dust.

I could picture her feel each soft top, a baby's fontanelle.
She'd wait patiently for them to be perfect, alone and ill.
Seeking the elusive scent of ripeness, sniffing each crown,
she'd pick up, sigh, reject, put gently down.

I leaned, pushed my hardest, that night in a dream,
on the door we failed to open on a stuffed full room.
The skin burst apart and I stepped into its hollow core
with pips as big as feet. So sweet so soft it was in there
where the juice dripped into my mouth. It was luscious,
a safe place for her, dark, perfectly spacious.

Time
How very near us stand the two vast gulfs of time, the past and the future, in which all things disappear. Marcus Aurelius, 'Meditations'

In the ancient Egyptian Book of the Dead,
That guidebook for the afterlife's travails,
an illustration recurs to depict
the passage of time. Here are two painted
lions, side view, back to back, their tails
striped, black tipped and elegantly flicked
about their haunches. Between them the sun
is rising from a stylised valley floor.
I guess this is the present: you are here.
Hieroglyphs beside them name each lion,
as they gaze out with arrogance, before,
and after, red-maned, lifelike yet austere.
One looks to the left, one to the right.
If you were naming them what would you write?

Perversely (to me), the lion who glares
right is named Yesterday, the other,
gazing left is Tomorrow. I suppose
I'm thinking of life as a path which wears
its track from left to right to the farther
side as these words do. Who knows
the mind of this painter who chose the names?
We are accustomed to the pilgrim's progress,
the winding road, the past trailing behind,
the journey with its waymarks and its aims.
Where is their present? Does that bold sun bless
that present day till dusk when it declines?
We chase hours and seconds that won't stay,
will our tomorrow's present last all day?

No, it has a nanosecond's sphere,
and our past we never shed with night.
It's made its mark, the scar upon my face,
the bruises on my heart, irrational fear.
The memory of blue hills, the wistful light
before us shines so plain, the happy place,
the one we can't return to, safe at last.
The future has just the one certain fact,
that chases us, is nearer every night.
I'm told when we are talking of the past
we look down, the future makes us react
by raising our eyes. To something out of sight?
Perhaps it is in hope we lift our head.
We cannot undo deeds or raise the dead.

The Ancient Greeks believed the past was spread
out before them, for it was the known;
in front, like Housman's longed for farms and spires.
The future skulked behind them, it waited
at their backs, where it hid fame, the lone
executioner, famine or the fires
of war or love. Then an old man could die,
his past before him, his glory or shame,
or just a patchwork of his ordinary days.
Today Andean peoples still apply
the past in front, future behind frame
when they speak of time, and their own way
of gesturing, over centuries, vast space,
mimes Socrates in Athens' market place.

Father

At the Walsingham shrine Our Lady is everywhere.
Her statue, richly dressed, crowned in gold, holds
up her baby. An Italian master's 'Virgin and Child
with a Red Rose' darkly glows. Joseph is nowhere.
Blue-robed in the souvenir shop, Mary hugs her infant
repeatedly in cheap statuettes. I hear: *But I want one*.
He pesters his mother like a child, the tall young man
who makes a rocking gesture, hands laced in front:
*Please, I want one with the **man** holding the baby.*
The assistant shakes her head. Mum leads him away.

It's the sight of his cradling that has me undone,
a sense of something lost on waking from a dream.
I don't remember him at all. I was only just one.
Surely he must have held me, rocked me to sleep?

It's not that I don't believe in ghosts

I just can't see them.
My mother could.
She saw a line of monks
cross a murky moor, then vanish.
She heard spectral children laughing
in empty rooms
at the Thomas Hardy Museum.
She stopped by the staircase
in East Riddlesden Hall,
sensing unhappy spirits.
Once, at dawn, she saw
her beloved friend
sitting at the foot of the bed.
'I'm just visiting,' said Hazel cheerfully.
The phone call came next day.

My mother didn't come to say goodbye
to me, but now she, too,
is on the other side of the thin wall
between semi-detached worlds,
can she still see down the alley
of the years?

She sees the four of us
in bright sunshine,
sitting on the wall outside St Paul's
in a row, youngest to oldest,
eating lettuce sandwiches, and hears again
that Irishwoman saying,
'It's a grand family you have there.'
Our mother holds out her arms
as the two in the middle jump down
and run to her.